A gift for
Rhonda

From
*Lisa
&
Family*

ANGELS EVERYWHERE by Lynn Valentine

This edition licensed to Hallmark Cards, Inc. by Premium Press America

Copyright © 1999 by Lynn Valentine

ISBN 1-887654-75-5

Hallmark SKU: BOK3045

www.hallmark.com

Editor Mardy Fones
Interior Design by Bob Bubnis/BookSetters—bksetters@aol.com

Printed in China
Second Edition 2001
10 11 12 13

Angels EVERYWHERE

MIRACLES & MESSAGES

BY LYNN VALENTINE

BOK 3045

GIFT BOOKS
from Hallmark

PREMIUM
PRESS
AMERICA

an-gel n. An immortal being attendant
          upon God; a very kind and
          lovable person; a helping or
          guiding spirit.

Table of Contents

Introduction

Do not forget to entertain strangers,
for by so doing some people have
entertained angels without knowing it.
—Hebrews 13:2 NIV

It's funny how you can go to church for years and years and never quite get it. Maybe you are like I was not all that long ago, where part of you believes and part of you wonders.

When I started this book, I did so planning to take it on more like a journalist studying the phenomena of Angel sightings. I dug into everything I could find — the Bible, books by Bible scholars, obscure books, out-of-print books, articles and even the Internet to learn as much as I could about these heavenly beings.

It wasn't until I began reading and interviewing those who claimed to have had encounters with Angels, that this book took on a new meaning for me. Suddenly, in that place where heart, intellect and spirit all meet, I knew that it was real.

It is my prayer that regardless of what you believe about Angels, that you will be inspired and turn the last page with a renewed hope. I know I have.

Yours Very Truly,

Lynn Valentine

Dedication

To God.

I'm no poet and I can hardly call myself a writer after the book you've written. But this work is dedicated to you. I pray you are thinking . . . "Well done, my good and faithful servant."

The angel of the Lord encamps around those who honor Him . . . and He delivers them.

—*Psalm 34:8*

Acknowledgement

In compiling this book and interviewing the witnesses to these events I was moved time and time again by the desire of these people to share their stories with the world. The stories that they regarded as private, personal and too fantastic to share became a testimony to them and almost the fulfillment of a life purpose to share these words and experiences with you.

As I talked with these people, friendships were born which I will take with me forever. I would like to acknowledge now the special contribution of the following people. . .

Maddy — Thanks for always re-charging my batteries with your enthusiasm.

Shirley—Thanks for helping me wrap this up in such a mighty way.

Andie — A friend and a poet. A diamond in the rough.

Sharon — Thank you for opening up your heart to share.

Deborah —Thank you for not leaving out the best part.

Donna — I will never be able to look at a butterfly the same again. (HUG)

Bob S. — Your story and example have inspired me to listen to my life, in hopes of someday hearing the music you hear..

George and Bette — Thanks for believing in me . . . AGAIN!

Thank you to my family for patiently waiting for mommy to finish.

Thank you, Mom, I do BELIEVE.

And special thanks to all of those who submitted their stories to share. Your selfless acts of kindness to be of help and encouragement take my breath away. God Bless You.

To my husband, Bob, the unsung HERO in my life.

"Be Calm"

On Jan. 17, 1994, a powerful earthquake jolted California. The magnitude 6.7 earthquake hit at 4:31 a.m. and caused severe damage throughout several communities, leaving many dead, hundreds of others injured and millions more frightened. The rumble was so loud in my townhouse that I couldn't hear the walls around me cracking or the plates and windows breaking and shattering.

Anyone who has ever been through a big quake will relate to the helpless feeling you have afterward. The feeling of not being able to trust the ground you are standing on is undescribable. After the initial shock and seeing the extensive damage all around me, I had to get used to the

constant aftershocks. Going upstairs to my bedroom terrified me. I, like many others, slept in my clothes with the
lights on.

In mid-March 1994, we went through a particularly violent aftershock sequence. We had seven strong aftershocks all before daylight.

During one of these, I was holding on to the headboard
of my bed, terrified as the bed violently shook. Suddenly,
through the roar of the earthquake, I heard a Booming
Voice saying, "Be Calm." The Voice was so loud that it
seemed the entire world should have heard it. It was a
deep authoritative voice, but unlike any voice I had ever
heard. It was coming from the corner of my room, near a
bookcase.

Upon hearing the Voice, I immediately felt a sense of
peace. I grabbed a piece of paper and wrote down the
words, "Be Calm." I placed the paper in a frame and put it
inside the nightstand next to my bed.

The next day, I called my Mother to tell her about the
voice. She thought it must have been an Angel or the
Voice of God.

The peace and serenity I felt stayed with me throughout other aftershocks. My friends in Los Angeles knew I
was afraid of earthquakes, so they would call me right

after the strong aftershocks to see if I was okay. Each time they noticed I was calm and several of them asked me why I was no longer so fearful. I told them about the Booming Voice saying, "Be Calm."

In April of 1997, I was planning to drive 225 miles north to Fresno for my uncle's 90th birthday party. The trip involved driving through the Tehachapi mountains and the Grapevine, an earthquake-prone region. I kept telling myself I'd have no problem driving through this mountain pass, unless there was an earthquake.

Around 4:45 a.m. on the day of my planned trip, we had another strong earthquake and the epicenter was in the exact area I had to drive through.

Even though the epicenter was about 45 miles from my home, it was felt quite strongly throughout the Los Angeles area, stirring up the old fears.

As the ground was still shaking, I reached to turn the light on. I opened the night stand to get my flashlight in case the electricity went out, but as I did, the framed "Be Calm" note I had written in the middle of the night three years earlier fell out and landed on the floor. My eyes fell upon those comforting words and I knew that my seeing them was no coincidence.

Reassured that God and His Angels were protecting me, I packed my car and drove to Fresno for my uncle's birthday party. Driving right over the epicenter of the quake that had just struck two hours before, I felt a sense of peace and tranquillity. I quit looking down at the earth and began looking up into the sky and the beautiful mountains that lay before me.

I no longer leave the framed "Be Calm" message inside my nightstand. It sits on top of it where I can see it daily.

—*Kathy Fjermedal*
Santa Monica,
California

Just Passing Through

The winter of 1994 had been unforgettable due to the vast amounts of snowfall and ice that had crippled our area for weeks. However, the beginning of March had given us promise of nicer weather as spring slowly inched its way around the corner, and winter's worst temper tantrums had gradually ceased leaving only cold mornings, frost and ice blanketing the vulnerable outdoors.

As a schoolteacher, I left early each morning for my 20-minute drive to school. My youngest son, Joshua, would accompany me since he attended the same school. This time to and from school became a time of bonding throughout the years, leaving precious memories.

Angels Everywhere

We had bought a van the summer before, but because of its extended top, we could not park it in our garage. On bitterly cold mornings, thick frost would form on my windows, forcing us to scrape them.

One morning as I was trying to scrape off a heavy coating of ice, my husband appeared in the driveway with a kettle of hot, steaming water and threw it on the front window of the van.

As my wipers raced back and forth, the ice magically vanished, but within seconds it crystallized again, leaving me frustrated. My husband became perturbed. He yelled for me to shut off the wipers, since he assumed they had caused the frost to reappear. He then got more hot water, and again, the ice miraculously melted.

"Don't turn your wipers on!" he ordered before going back inside. So, slowly down the driveway Josh and I ventured that dark, shivering cold morning. As I carefully crept out onto our street that led to the highway, a glaze of ice began to dance across my windshield; nevertheless, I still could slightly manage to see the road.

Realizing my windshield was crystallizing, Josh asked if I could see. I replied "barely" and with the defrosters still on high, I switched on my wipers hoping the ice would dissipate faster. By then, I had slowly driven out onto the highway. In horror, the condition worsened within seconds. The crystals became a thick opaque coat of milky white ice. Josh, this time screamed, "Mom, can you see?" A "no" I groaned. Except for a tiny peephole at the bottom of the windshield where the wipers had rested seconds ago, I was blind.

I began to tremble, knowing that we were headed for trouble. I knew that I needed to pull off the highway, but I could not see the road. My speed had diminished to a crawl. I was aware that I also could not see traffic behind me, around me or in front of me.

Suddenly, Josh yelled, "Mom, look at the light!"

I looked up from my peephole and saw through a glazed windshield a light so bright that it reminded me of train lights.

Shaking, I screamed out to Josh, "My God, he's on our side of the highway!"

"No, Mom, I think you are on his side!" he blurted out in terror.

The white line I had thought was the edge of the road was really the dividing line. Aloud, I pleaded with God and my guardian Angel to help me NOW! A blaring horn intensified my fear. I knew if I were in the wrong lane and pulled to the right, I might end up in the path of a car. I only had a fraction of a second to make my choice. Slowly, hoping any cars in that lane would allow me in, I eased my van to the right.

My body stiffened as I whispered, "Spare my son, God; please spare my son!" At that moment, a gush of wind rocked the van. Pebbles pelted its side. The lights that were upon us were overwhelming in brightness. Although the windows were up, a gust of wind passed through our vehicle. As our tires finally left the pavement and rolled slowly onto the shoulder, my body loosened, muscles began to shake and tears of thankfulness rolled down my cold cheeks.

We were safe! I looked out to see what I had just missed only to see the black of the night staring me in the face.

To the passenger side of our van came a pounding and a familiar voice.

"Shirley, Shirley, are you all right?" My neighbor Gail pulled in behind me.

She said she was driving a few car lengths from me and had watched the nightmare unfold. She went on to tell me that the vehicle that was upon us was an 18-wheeler.

Angels Everywhere

As she questioned why I had been on "his" side of the road, I pointed to my windshield and explained briefly my error. Realizing I was in no condition to drive, she instructed me to remain in my van, and she would return shortly with my husband.

Later that evening, Gail called me to discuss once more my near-death experience. At the end of our conversation, she explained that she was hesitant to call me, but wanted to tell me what she had witnessed.

"You didn't make it, Shirley. I saw everything clearly, since I was behind you. You didn't make it, girl," she kept insisting.

"I don't understand, Gail. I did make it. God must have heard my cry or my Guardian Angel lost a few feathers on this one," I tried to jest.

"No, Shirley," she said, "I distinctly saw the semi-truck going through the side of your van as you tried pulling off the road. I could hardly believe what I was seeing, but I did see it. You didn't make it."

I was stunned and speechless as she spoke. I knew, too, that the good Lord did hear my soul cry out on that cold, dark morning and gave us another chance for life. Why? I don't know. I just know now beyond the shadow of doubt, that there is someone watching us.

Angels Everywhere

For years I have believed in Guardian Angels. In fact, I named mine long ago (Constance), because he is constantly watching over me.

Thank you, Constance, for allowing us to pass through!

—Shirley Lakes
Shepherdsville,
Kentucky

My Angel

When I was little, we lived in an old two-story farm house with a steep staircase. It had a landing about halfway up before it angled off and went the rest of the way to the second floor.

I was playing with my toys one afternoon, but eventually became bored and decided to go see what my mother was doing. As I hurried down the stairs, I lost my footing and began to fall.

That's when I saw someone standing on the landing. He was big and powerful looking and his frame shimmered. Although I probably would scream now if it happened again, I was not afraid at the time. Watching the light dance and swirl about him was comforting like the soothing glow of a fireplace.

I realized then I was seeing an Angel.

As I watched him, I suddenly realized that I was not falling, but floating very slowly toward him. It was like I was moving in slow motion.

"Don't be afraid," he said, "everything is going to be okay."

I drifted downward, as if I were being carried, until finally my feet came softly to the floor.

After I touched down, I looked up and saw that the Angel had vanished.

I went to tell my mom. When I said I had fallen down the stairs, she was worried at first, but became perplexed when she saw I was fine.

"What happened?" she asked.

"My Angel helped me."

I told her the whole story, but I don't think she believed me then.

Years later, my mom and I were talking about Angels, and I brought up the encounter I had as a child. This time my age and the clarity of my recollection convinced her that on that day, my Guardian Angel really had stepped in to save me from injury.

As we wondered what God might have been sparing me from, my brother Aaron jumped in to share his theory about my experience.

Angels Everywhere

He thinks that because I am a dancer and I do routines with a Christian message, that I was caught so I could dance for God.

It makes me feel like dancing just thinking about that.

—*Sarah Loutner*
Springfield, Tennessee

He will give His angels charge of you,
to guard you in all your ways.

—Psalm 91:11

Angel on Flight 1641

Everything had happened so fast. The ad in the magazine detailing the weekend seminar in Sedona, Arizona. The call to my travel agent. Flight reservations to Phoenix. Car rental arrangements for the 120-mile drive. Motel accommodations. Getting time off work during our busiest season and finding I had enough money to afford this spur-of-the-moment trip. This was certainly out of character for me. I never did anything on the spur of the moment.

I detested the monotony of car trips. My immediate comfort zone never takes me more than 35 miles in any direction. But here I was, sitting in seat 25D on Northwest Flight #1641, waiting for take-off.

Angels Everywhere

My thoughts were interrupted by a heated discussion in the seats next to me. The occupants, an elderly couple, were having a disagreement about seating. They wound up moving across the aisle to other seats, only to create more commotion when the rightful occupants of those seats showed up. One of the young men took the window seat in my row, leaving the seat between us vacant. I don't know where his companion ended up, as my thoughts were now focusing on something altogether different.

Were the walls really closing in on me? Why was it so difficult to catch my breath? I felt like screaming, but couldn't. My heart was beating so quickly and loudly, I felt as if it would jump out of my chest at any moment. All I could think of was getting OFF THE PLANE — but my legs would not move — and the aisle was completely blocked by boarding passengers. What was I going to do? I just had to get off that plane.

I dug my fingernails into the armrests of my seat, as if this could somehow help me hold on to reality. But it only magnified the horror. How could I have been so incredibly stupid as to forget my fear of flying?

The last time I'd flown — seven years ago on a nonstop from Honolulu — the plane had taken a sudden drop in altitude too terrifying for words.

Drinks, snacks, stewardesses and unbuckled passengers were sent flying.

Even though the pilot assured us it was "just a little bit of unexpected turbulence," I'd vowed never to fly again. But here I sat, trapped on a plane still sitting at the gate, scared witless.

My racing thoughts were interrupted by a calm voice asking if the seat next to me was taken. Without looking up, I nodded and mumbled something about my being a white-knuckled flyer.

The voice responded, "I know," as baggage was being stowed in the overhead compartment. *Was it really that obvious?* I wondered.

As he seated himself, I noticed we were both wearing pale purple shirts.

How synchronistic, I thought, but said nothing, as I was still very much absorbed by my fear-of-flying mode. The next thing I knew he pried my nails away from the armrest and gently took my hand between his. Under other circumstances, I would have protested this obvious infringement of my space — but somehow this was different.

At first his words seemed to be coming from somewhere far away, and I could barely make them out. But it didn't take me long to tune in to what he was telling me.

Angels Everywhere

He gave me a detailed rundown of what was going on in the cockpit, assured me of the safety of the plane, alluded to his innumerable trips on just this type of aircraft, and explained each creak, bump, grind and shimmy the plane made — almost before it happened. I was still in no condition to respond verbally, so I just kept nodding, at once indicating I understood what he was saying as well as encouraging him to keep talking.

He ordered a glass of Chablis for each of us. I eagerly accepted and at last could feel myself relaxing. Once I got my wits about me, I noticed my rescuer was a very attractive man. He had a mischievous twinkle in his eye and the most sincere smile I'd ever seen. Soon we were talking a mile-a-minute about practically every subject under the sun. In what seemed like no time at all, the pilot was giving us our landing instructions.

I thanked the helpful stranger for his kindness, and as we parted in the terminal, we shared an embrace only friends of long-standing would find comfortable.

In a moment he was gone. Only then did it occur to me that I didn't even know his name. I returned to the plane and asked the stewardess what the name of the gentleman seated next to me was. She looked at her manifest and with a puzzled expression said, "But ma'am, there was no one seated next to you. The manifest shows that seat flew empty."

A chill ran down my spine, and I smiled knowingly. It didn't really matter if I didn't know his name. I'd seen *Highway to Heaven* and *Touched By An Angel* enough times to believe the TV characters just might have real-world counterparts. And besides, who else would know the intricacies of flying better than the Angel seated next to me on Northwest Flight #1641?

—*Ilsa Troge*
Santa Rosa, California

Angels are speaking to all of us—
Some of us are only listening better.

—*Anonymous*

His Love For His Children

As a small child, I was once sick in bed and felt I was suffocating. I looked up and over to the head of my bed and saw a glowing figure sitting very close to me. Somehow, I knew that was my Guardian Angel! Later in life, my mother told me that I had been very ill with pneumonia, to the point where I was given the last rites. Knowing that, I now believe that my Angel protected me from death.

When I was in my 30s, my husband became suddenly and seriously ill.

I was sitting alone in the hospital waiting room. I was feeling very downhearted and afraid I would be left a widow at this young age. I was trying to pray to God when an elderly lady sat right next to me. Because the room was basically empty, she could have had any chair she wanted.

I exchanged the basic pleasantries with her, but I really didn't feel like talking. She kept chatting, and then, in the midst of our conversation, she suddenly locked eyes with me. I've never seen such blue eyes, and she held me with them. It was like she was looking down into my soul. She said, "Everything will be all right — just let go and let God." She got up to leave, and the next minute she just wasn't there at all.

My husband did recover and is still alive today.

❦

This year, I became seriously ill with chest pains. During this time, I had to make a week-long business trip to Texas.

My husband was concerned about me being alone, but I insisted I would be all right and went on ahead.

The week passed relatively pain free, and I prepared to leave. I had to return the rental car, then take the shuttle to the main terminal to check my baggage. As I started to carry my luggage to the shuttle bus, I became very fatigued and felt twinges in my chest. The shuttle bus door opened, and I saw that there were three very steep stairs up to the on-board luggage rack. I looked at those stairs and doubted I could lift my baggage up to the rack.

About that time, I heard a voice say, "Let me help you with that," and I turned to see a handsome young man dressed in a beautiful camel coat, white vest, camel scarf and brown pants. He had reddish hair and really looked great. I smiled at him, and all of a sudden, my luggage was in the rack! Understand that he did NOT board the shuttle to place my luggage in the rack. I looked at the luggage and turned to thank him and could not see him anywhere. There were very few people in the area, and I couldn't figure out how he disappeared within a matter of seconds.

Shortly thereafter, I had open heart surgery because the main artery in my heart was blocked. The day before my operation, my doctor told me if I had exerted myself into a heart attack, I would have dropped dead. It was then I realized that the young man was not REALLY a man at all, but an Angel that God had sent to save my life.

> —*Kathy Ozanne*
> *Thornton, Colorado*

If you pray truly, you will feel within yourself a great assurance, and the angels will be your companions.

—*Evagrius of Pontus*

Angel at the Beach

One very hot weekend, I decided to take my two daughters to the beach to cool off. We were playing in the sand, building sand castles and making memories, when all of the sudden, a huge wave came up, catching us by surprise and knocking us down. Before I could get to my feet, another wave, even larger than the first, crashed over us.

Frantically, I fought my way to my knees, while grabbing my 3-year-old. I could see my 5-year-old trying to get back on her feet, but she was scooped up by the water and pulled farther from me. I was able to grab the end of her hair, but she must have swallowed some water, because she had blacked out.

Angels Everywhere

With my 3-year-old in one arm, and my other hand tied up holding on to my other daughter, it was like one of those tug-of-war matches. With each surge of the tide, I was being pulled across the line.

❧

Then out of nowhere came this boy. Even though my daughter was under the water and out of sight, he quickly found her. He looked to be around 10 years old, but he grabbed her up with such calmness and confidence that I released her into his care and watched as he brought her quickly to shore.

I managed to get to my older daughter's side. In seconds, she began coughing up water and regained her consciousness. I had not yet caught my own breath as I began crying. I couldn't believe how short of a time it could take to lose a loved one.

What could have happened had the boy not come in time . . . *wait, where is the boy?*

He was gone. He didn't wait around to be thanked. He didn't wait for a reward.

I looked for him and asked others if they had seen him, but nobody knew what I was talking about. He disappeared —

Angels Everywhere

just like that.   I did not think anything of it until I came home that night. As I was praying and thanking God, I realized that that was not a normal circumstance.   That was an Angel.

—*Marfi Barnes*
Long Beach, California

If we ever wish to know angels for what they truly are . . .
perhaps it is we who must first learn to fly.

—*Anonymous*

An Angel Visit

My father died in January 1996. It was my first major experience with death.

I was the oldest of seven children in what could be described as a pretty familiar brood of Irish Catholics in the '60s. While we were each loved as individuals, it was a common perception that I was a Daddy's girl. Even well into adulthood, this perception continued.

After my father's death, I had to return to the ordinary chores of life and the routine of my job. With my body on automatic and my mind in neutral, I put one foot in front of the other and went through the motions.

One day, as I pushed the shopping cart through the aisles of my favorite food store, I was distracted from my thoughts by the sound of a whimpering child running toward me. I can still see her long, curly red hair as she passed.

As the well-trained eldest daughter, I wanted to reach out and comfort her. But as a woman in recovery, I knew I could not save every crying child. The whimpering 10-year-old would have to find comfort from another.

At the end of the next aisle, she reappeared. This time there was no battle within me.

"Honey, what's wrong? Are you lost? Hold on to my basket." I never did touch her or guide her hand, yet she stopped and took hold of the front of my shopping cart. I continued to ask, "Did you lose your Mommy?"

"No," she said, "I lost my Daddy."

I felt a lump in my throat and I wanted to cry out, "I just lost my Daddy, too." Instead I smiled and said, "Come on, Honey, we'll go look for him."

I can still hear myself offering assurances several times in our strolling, "Don't worry, Honey, he won't leave you here. He won't leave the store without you. He's right here somewhere. We'll find him."

As soon as I said that, she took off running. It was as if she had suddenly seen him and vanished around the corner.

Angels Everywhere

I strolled passed the checkout lines, looking for them. Nothing.

Again, I walked through, searching for the bright red locks of hair. There were only six short lines.

How could they have disappeared so quickly?

She was gone.

Some folks might disagree with me, and think I was making something out of nothing, but I believe she was an Angel. Looking back, I believe that little girl was God's messenger sent to be with me—to move with me through another step of grief toward healing.

—*Madeline J. Hartwell*
Hansen, Idaho

Death is not a period, only a comma.

— *Sign outside a country church*

The Accident that Never Was

I t was Christmas Eve, and I was driving to a friend's
house during the hectic Los Angeles rush hour. The
night was pitch black, and it was raining so hard that vis-
ibility was nil. The three lanes of traffic on congested La
Cienega Boulevard were stopped for a red light, and my
tiny white sports car was the last in a very long line of
vehicles. I was in the far left lane, wedged next to a 2-foot
high cement island. I casually looked in my rear-view mirror at the shiny wet street behind me when I saw three cars
speeding behind me. There was one in each lane racing
toward the stopped traffic, exceeding the speed where they
could safely stop. The cars suddenly slammed on their
brakes and started sliding and swerving all over the road.

Angels Everywhere

I knew for certain that my car would be hit and having no way to escape it, murmured, "Please, God, help me," as I braced for the impact. I kept looking in the mirror and watching the cars approach. Unexpectedly, I felt a very gentle tap at the back of my car followed by a slight lifting sensation—but did not see a car hit me. I then heard the crash of the cars slamming into each other. I waited a few moments for the dust to settle and then got out to see what had happened and give assistance if anyone needed help.

I was surprised to find my car sitting on the cement island. I had not felt enough of an impact to have moved that far, plus the car was exactly parallel to its original position, as if it had been lifted and moved three or four feet to the left then set gently down. It seemed slightly strange, but at the time I really didn't give it much thought.

Fortunately, no one was physically hurt. However, there was considerable damage to several of the stopped cars and the three cars that had hit them. What amazed me was that everyone wanted to know how I was and how much damage my car had suffered. I said I was fine, and that nothing had happened to me or my car, as I had not been hit. With that statement, several people stared at me in disbelief, asking, "What do you mean nothing happened to you? We saw your car fly through the air! You got hit harder than anyone else here!"

We then walked around my car and observed that there was not one scratch or mark on it. We also realized that the position of my car was against all possible laws of physics.

I was thankful that there were so many witnesses to this incident, as it opened my eyes to the miracle that had just taken place. From my perspective, nothing happened. After they explained what they had seen from their perspectives, I realized that someone had protected me by lifting my car out of harm's way. Although I did not see or hear anything, I know the gentle tap and lift that I felt had to have been from my Guardian Angel.

—Troika Celeste Germain
Mount Shasta,
California

"There is rejoicing in the presence of the angels of God over one sinner who repents."

— *Luke 15:10* NIV

The Happiest Day

My mother was an invalid when she passed away. Her strength and vitality had been eroded by the passage of time, but she had a strong spirit and that kind of strength that comes from a certain knowledge that life here on earth is nothing more than a prelude for what is ahead. Still though, despite her infirmities, her death was completely unexpected.

She seemed so alive to me, so it was difficult for me to be suddenly without her. To make matters worse, my brother was in the military and far away, leaving just me to deal with all of the details. In the midst of all of the funeral arrangements, I would cry out to God, asking Him for help — for strength and comfort and peace of mind. Still, I had no relief.

Even in the midst of my prayer time, I could not sense that He was anywhere close by. I basically felt alone. My mom was gone, and now God seemed to be gone too.

I contacted my brother and scheduled the funeral for as late possible, but it was still doubtful he would make it.

Then came the time to deal with choosing the music. Mom had told me weeks before she passed that she wanted a particular song played at her funeral. It was called, "My God and I."

The music director agreed to sing it and the morning of the funeral, my brother did manage to get there. Still, even as the funeral was in progress, I was struggling with God and this feeling that he had not come through for me.

Then something marvelous happened. As the vocalist began to sing, I started listening to the words and taking in the beauty of it all.

I looked out over the markers and the neatly cut lawn to see something incredible.

There, off in the distance, I saw Mom. She was holding the hand of an Angel, and he was leading her away. Her legs were strong again — the infirmities were gone.

Angels Everywhere

She did not look back at those of us who were left behind. I suppose she was far too excited about what lay ahead —after all, she was about to have the happiest day of her life.

—Ruth Busby
Goodletsville,
Tennessee

Some things are true,
whether you believe them, or not.

— Nathaniel Messenger
City of Angels

Stranded

I am a trucker, and on one cold night after an ice storm in Lansing, Michigan, I had an encounter with an Angel.

The roads were hazardous, so I followed another truck on our way to make a grocery store warehouse delivery. I had only been there once before, so I was trying to keep up with him, but somehow I managed to lose him anyway.

I spotted our exit and got off the freeway, but my partner was nowhere in sight. Thinking I had a pretty good idea of where I was going, I took a left, but soon I was lost. Calling my partner on the CB radio, I learned that I had undershot the road I needed to take and had miles to go before I could get back on track.

Angels Everywhere

Distressed, I began looking for a place to turn around, but the streets just got darker and more ice-covered as I went along. I found myself in an industrial area that had not seen a salt truck all night long. Finally, I came across an empty intersection that looked wide enough to get my big rig going the other way.

Wrong.

I was on solid ice, and, after several minutes of maneuvering, I ended up being stuck with no way to go backward or forward. I was alone and miles away from any help. Looking up I said, "God, you could really help me if you wanted to!"

As soon as I uttered that prayer, a salt truck appeared out of nowhere. He salted the road all around me and even got out and gave hand signals to keep me out of the roadside ditch as I got back in the right direction.

I rounded the corner and was so happy to finally be back on my way. I pulled over to the side of the road to thank him.

The salt truck was gone.

Not so much as 15 seconds had elapsed since I saw him, and I could easily see more than a half mile in every direction, but he had vanished.

Angels Everywhere

I initially thought it was odd that a salt truck would be out so far away from traveled streets, but once it disappeared, I remembered my prayer to the Almighty and realized that I wasn't stranded after all.

—*Mike Harrington*
Warrenville, Illinois

I saw the tracks of angels in the earth. The beauty of heaven walking by itself on the world.

— *Petrarch*

My One-Eyed Angel

I t was during the Christmas holidays, and my husband, two children and I went shopping in a larger city 100 miles away. There we met my sister and her husband. We had a lot of shopping and visiting ahead of us, but were not in a hurry and planned to make a day of it. It was 11 p.m. when we finally started for home, tired but happy.

We were still 36 miles from home when it began to snow quite furiously. The closer we got to home, the worse the roads were. The snow was coming down so hard we had trouble staying in our lane of the highway. My husband slowed to 10 miles an hour, but still we had problems staying on the road. Unable to see the road and distinguish it from the ditches and canyons, I began to pray for God to send His Angels to help us. I picked up our cellular phone and called my sister. They had made it home to another town with no problems. I asked for them to pray for us. She and her husband immediately knelt and prayed for our safety.

By now my husband's eyes were tired of straining, and we were weaving all over the road. It seemed we were the only ones on the road so late. Suddenly, from a distance behind, I spotted a single headlight. It was coming toward us at a remarkable speed considering the road conditions and heaviness of the snow falling. In a moment it was right behind us. I told my husband that someone else must be just as insane as we were. Then around us came the light.

Where it passed, it left a set of tire tracks, steady and true for us to follow. It traveled faster than we could keep up with, and soon it was out of sight. Still, even though snow was coming down heavily, the tires tracks left behind by the light remained free and clear. We followed them for several miles. The snow stopped falling so hard and we picked up speed.

Just as quickly as the headlight had appeared, the tracks suddenly ended. No turning, no exiting, no pulling off to the side, these tracks just ended—as if the vehicle had lifted off the ground. I looked at my husband and told him I knew who was driving ahead of us. He looked at me in surprise and asked me who it was. I told him it was one of our Guardian Angels. He shook his head affirmatively as we pulled into our drive. We both thanked God for our safe arrival and for giving us our Guardian Angel. Even if it only had one eye.

—*Nola Jones*
Fargo, North Dakota

To love for the sake of being loved is human, but to love for the sake of loving is angelic.

—*Alphonse de Lamartine*

A Mother's Love

My mother had suffered from diabetes, kidney failure and finally cancer of the colon. She passed away with my two older brothers and me by her bedside.

As she took her last breaths I thought to myself, *How could I go on through life without this wonderful lady who had nurtured me into the man that I had become?*

Approximately three months after we buried Mom, I was looking through the window, feeling terribly lonely and depressed. I must have sat there for hours.

As I sat there, I drifted off to sleep and dreamed I was walking down this road. I looked to my left at a beautiful field and saw a large tree about 100 yards away. As I kept looking at this tree I saw a brilliant white light move from behind it. I was amazed at the brightness. I felt attracted to it and started walking toward it. It looked like a diamond reflecting the sun, throwing off beams of color all around. When I got about 15 yards away, the light subsided and I saw my mother's face. She had a white gown on and looked beautiful. Before she passed away, Mom had one of her legs amputated from the diabetes, but she had both legs now. She smiled and looked at me and held her arms out to hug me.

As she wrapped her arms around me, she said, "I love you and I know you love me, but you have to go on with your life and be there for the people that depend on you. I have been preparing you for this all your life."

She also said that she was fine, and that her father, sister and brother and others who preceded her in death were there taking good care of her.

She slowly moved backward, looking so peaceful and serene, until the light again enveloped her. I watched the light until I could no longer see it.

At the precise moment the light disappeared, I was awakened by a noise at the front door. I got up to see if someone was there and found the screen door wide open. I immediately noticed there was no one around and that

Angels Everywhere

there was not so much as a breath of wind at all to blow it open. I knew without a doubt that Mom was leaving and this was to show me that I wasn't dreaming.

—*Mike La Broi*
Gary, Indiana

In the arms of the angel . . .
May you find some comfort here.

—*Sarah McLachlan*
From her song "Angel"

Are You Still Mad?

About a week after my son was killed in an accident, I decided to go to one of the Alcoholics Anonymous meetings he'd been attending. I planned to talk to them about drinking and driving. It seemed like the right thing to do. I had so much that I wanted to say . . . so much hurt to get out.

I told them I was angry with God—that I had told Him not to speak to me anymore, and that I wasn't speaking to Him.

I left the room not feeling any better and started back home.

I decided to go to the local K-Mart while I was out and cut over to a side street as a short cut.

65

Angels Everywhere

It was a similar street to the one my boy was killed on.

As I drove, I thought about this and about the meeting. Suddenly, I looked up to see red flashing lights in front of me. I slammed on the brakes and skidded to a halt only about six feet from the semi-truck ahead of me.

A voice said to me, "This is what happened to your son. He did not see the truck. Are you still mad?"

I immediately pulled to the side of the road and apologized to God. I knew He had sent an Angel.

—*Donna Theisen*
Fort Myers, Florida

GUARDIAN ANGEL PRAYER

Angel of God, my guardian dear,

To whom God's love commits me here.

Ever this day be at my side,

To light and guard, to rule and guide.

—*Author unknown*

"The more materialistic science becomes, the more angels shall I paint: their wings are my protest in favor of the immortality of the soul."

—*Sir Edward Coley Burne-Jones*

The Ushering

S tella Margaret Heck was a saintly woman. She was the daughter of a Methodist preacher, a firm believer and a true example of a Proverbs 31 type of woman. At 90 years old, she was a witness to everyone, and, as a grandmother, she was an especially inspiring person to me.

Tragically, she fell ill in the spring of 1985. There was nothing they could do for her but help manage her pain and wait.

The pain was great, too. Thankfully, she was unconscious most of the time, but on those few occasions when she did awaken, her eyes told the story of suffering in ways that words could not fully describe.

Angels Everywhere

On Easter Sunday, about 5 a.m., I was awakened by a breeze. It was more than a breeze really, growing to a wind. This wind was not coming from a window but rather from the wall behind my bed.

The wind grew in intensity, and I became fully awake. I kept my eyes closed as I enjoyed the sensation of having this warm fragrant wind rushing over me. It was powerful but not violent. Strong and yet soft at the same time.

As I lay there, I can't say how I knew, but I realized that something special was happening, something holy.

I opened my eyes and saw this light gold mist riding the wind. And then, in the midst of the wind, I was able to make out the barely visible, translucent outlines of huge powerful wings. They did not have feathers as you see in paintings, but clearly, they were wings. They had a silver sheen to them with highlights of gold.

I knew right then these were Angels, taking her to heaven.

—*Rebecca Brown*
Springfield, Tennessee

Kelly

Kelly had just had her fourth birthday shortly before the car accident. She was everything to our family — the glue that had held us all together. We didn't know that until we lost her.

We had just dropped off my other two daughters at school and were on our way home when the car was broadsided by four cars. She wasn't wearing a seatbelt—this was back in 1971 before it was law—and ended up with severe injuries.

She never woke up.

She was in St. Mary's Hospital in the ICU for eight days before the doctors unplugged the life supports.

Angels Everywhere

One night, soon after, I woke up and saw a light in the doorway. Sitting up in bed, I saw Kelly standing there.

"Mommy, don't be afraid," she said. "I'm all right."

My eyes filled with tears as the agony poured out.

"You can't come with me now, but someday we'll be together again. Don't cry anymore, Mommy. I love you."

Kelly turned and vanished into the arms of waiting Angels.

—Linda Darlene
South Gate, California

Every time a bell rings, it means that an angel got his wings.

—*It's A Wonderful Life*

"For He shall give his angels charge over thee to keep thee in all thy ways."

—*Psalms 91:11*

Go to the Light

I had just arrived at my school around 7:30 a.m. when our school secretary paged me over the intercom for an important message. Had my husband locked himself out of the house again? Could a parent of one of my students be calling this early? These thoughts and more flooded my mind as I raced down each hall to the main office.

Upon entering, I realized something must be seriously wrong by the look on our secretary's face. I braced myself as she said without hesitating, "Go home, Shirley. Your father is dying." As my eyes teared and overflowed, I began to realize that the event that I had dreaded my whole lifetime was now becoming a reality.

Angels Everywhere

My father had been 42 when my twin sister and I were born. At an early age, I increasingly became conscious that my dad appeared to always be the oldest father among parents who accompanied their children to school functions. Sometimes a few of my friends would question, "Is that your grandpa or dad?" Eventually, I became very alarmed about Dad's age; as I entered high school, apprehension about still having my father upon graduation clouded my thoughts. He would be almost 60! My worrying was needless, for he had seen me graduate high school, and it had been 17 years since I earned my master's degree. I had been given an abundance of treasured years with him.

With tears streaming down my face, my heart pounded nervously as I rushed home to gather my family and head off for my hometown and my father's side.

For years, I had dreamed of being the one to help him depart this world without fear, for Dad had not been a Christian or spoken much of God until these last few years. Thankfully, little signs from him told me he had started a closer walk with Him.

In silence, my husband drove the three hours to Vincennes while I silently prayed for God to allow me to see and speak once more with my father before he died.

Angels Everywhere

Since my father had wrestled with two previous bouts of pneumonia that year, his strength and resistance were low. Just the night before, I had chatted with him long distance after discovering he had returned to the hospital. He assured me there was nothing to worry about.

"Sissy, I'll still be here this weekend. You can come up then," was his soft reply. We talked and laughed for nearly an hour, and I honestly felt that I would have that weekend to be near him once more.

As I dashed down the halls of the hospital to Intensive Care, my twin greeted me. She informed me of his perilous condition and how the doctors and staff had desperately worked trying to raise his blood pressure which had dangerously dropped. His condition quickly deteriorated.

Quietly entering his room, I could see life-support machines by his bed and a ventilator which prevented him from speaking. Though it allowed him to breathe, it painfully robbed him of his last words to me.

I sat tensely beside him taking his frail hand in mine, patting it and announcing that I was by his side now. I looked deep into his hazel eyes and knew the candle was burning out.

I talked to him for a brief time, just the two of us alone in the sanitized room of humming machines, the thread that allowed him to still be a part of this world. I knew God had generously allowed me this extra moment to talk to him. I gently kissed his cool brow and whispered, "Dad, do you know you're dying?"

Looking tenderly into my eyes and trying to smile, he nodded *yes* and gazed at the foot of his bed. Trying to ease any fears he may have, I once more squeezed Dad's hand and whispered, "Dad, God is here and loves you. He will lead you over to the other side. Don't be afraid."

Excitedly, he tried to raise up and pointed adamantly to the foot of his bed. He tried to say something but the ventilator prevented him. "Dad, is someone here?" Repeatedly, he pointed to the foot of his bed and nodded *yes*.

I began to tremble, for I knew what would very soon take place. There were only two of us in that room; however, my Dad's three dimensions were now four.

I motioned for the nurse to hurry and gather the family. As they rushed to his bedside, I looked down at my father and realized by the gray glaze over his eyes that he had quietly slipped into a coma. For the next few moments, his beloved family stood by his bed and watched the now useless machines slowly register the life that was withdrawing from my father's still body. As the last level dropped to zero, my twin cried out, "Fight, Dad! Stay with us! Fight!"

Angels Everywhere

I patted his lifeless hand and whispered, "Go to the light, Dad. It's all right. Go with Him to the light."

I could picture the Angel who awaited him at the foot of the bed, leading my father home.

> —*Shirley Lakes*
> *Shepherdsville,*
> *Kentucky*

God always has an angel of help for those who are willing to do their duty.

—*T. L. Cuyler*

The Acts Angel

We loved our little conservative church. My husband was a respected deacon there, and I headed up women's groups and Bible studies. We had been active in nearly every committee and had a hand in almost every stage of the church's growth over the years, making wonderful friends all along the way. If anyone would have told me that I was going to be torn away from my comfort zone there, I would have laughed at them.

One day, as I was making the bed, I collapsed onto it and found myself unable to move. I sensed that I wasn't alone, but the pressure over my body kept me from turning my head. I struggled against the force and eventually managed to position myself to see who was with me.

Angels Everywhere

There in the corner was an Angel. It was huge and was not contained by the room—its flowing mass went beyond the ceiling, floor and walls.

In its hands were two flaming swords going back and forth. As they swung, the Angel spoke, saying over and over, "Acts 1:8, Acts 1:8, Acts 1:8 . . ."

I don't know how long the experience lasted, but when the Angel vanished I got to my feet and scrambled for a Bible to find out what it said in Acts 1:8.

"You shall receive power when the Holy Spirit has come upon you and you shall be witnesses to Me in Jerusalem . . . and to the end of the earth."

I knew then and there that I needed to find a church where this scripture wasn't just read but was lived.

—*Ruth Busby*
Goodletsville,
Tennessee

Go Back

I was in an auto accident in 1980. I was driving home with my date when we were rear ended. Upon impact, I was temporarily paralyzed and my back was broken to the point where two disks needed to be removed.

Before surgery, they administered a myelogram, injecting dye into the spine to create an image for the surgeon to study. For some reason though, I had a bad reaction to the chemicals they used—which I believe caused me to die.

I watched from above as the medical team went into action, trying to resuscitate me. Nurses were slapping my face and hands, reporting to the doctor that my temperature was dropping.

Angels Everywhere

I remember thinking that it was strange that I should be watching all of this, and I wondered how it was possible that I could be airborne above them.

While in the air, an Angel came up beside me and in a soft voice said, "You must go back."

At the time, I was a single mother raising two daughters alone. I thought of them as the voice spoke again, "Your job is not yet complete, you must go back."

A few hours later, I awoke.

My mom told me that the doctors nearly lost me. Had it not been for the advice of an Angel, they would have.

—Judy G. Smith
Gladwin, Michigan

Hospital Visitor

I was in the hospital after being treated for my second heart attack. I was very depressed, feeling alone and scared. I did not want to die; there were so many things I wanted to do.

I was confined to bed, sorting through my fears, when a woman walked in. She was dressed in a hospital gown with a white satin robe over it, tied at the waist.

"I hear you are afraid of dying," she said.

I hadn't mentioned to anyone the internal struggle I was feeling.

"I just came by to tell you that you are going to be all right. You have not accomplished your purpose yet."

"I sure would like to know what that purpose is," I replied.

"It is something that is going to help a lot of people."

She paused, letting her words sink in and then said, "Everything will be okay."

There was something comforting in her voice, as if she really knew that what she said was the truth. Then with a reassuring smile she left.

I decided she must be a patient from a nearby room and later, asked my nurse about her. The nurse replied that nobody bearing my description was on the floor.

I did recover but wondered afterward just what my purpose was.

In 1995, my son died. After his death, I began writing a book about losing a child. I had to save my sanity and make his death count for something. I interviewed many others who had lost children, and I became a published author when it was all said and done.

My books have helped a lot of people make their way through the grieving process, and I have counseled many moms who have lost their children as well, helping to bring hope where there had been a broken heart.

I remember the words of that Angel who came to my hospital room and foretold what was to come.

I know what my purpose is now and will do what I was left here to do until she comes back to take me home.

—Donna Theisen
Ft. Myers, Florida

Some don't believe in miracles.
They say, "What happens is by chance"
They rush through God's creation,
Without a passing glance.

But for those that look and listen
throughout each precious day
They will find the tracks of Angels,
as they move along their way!

—*Andie Hellem*

Backseat Angel

About two weeks ago, I prayed God would reveal Himself to me.

Not long after making that prayer, I was off to work on a Friday morning. I was cruising along at around 65 mph, when I was jolted from my thoughts by the sight of a 4 X 4 piece of lumber in the road. I swerved hard to miss it but nicked it just enough to see it fly up between a semi-truck and a van right behind me. I heard it hit my car but was glad to see I had made it through what could have been a real disaster.

As my rapid heartbeat began to slow down, the truck driver came up beside me, got my attention and let me know that I really needed to stop and take a look at the side of my car. As soon as I could, I pulled over to find that the wooden post I nearly ran over had caused my rim to roll up away from the tire. Still, it had remained inflated. With just a few miles left to go, I went on to work, dropping the car off at a nearby service station.

When I got there, the garage owner said that in 50 years of service, he had never seen such badly damaged tires stay inflated.

Minutes after pulling in, the tire blew.

I realized then that I had heard, loud and clear, an answer to my prayer. God was there, and that day, He had one of His Angels in my back seat.

—V. Easely
Raleigh, North Carolina
Courtesy of He Invites,
Inc.

My Sunday Angel

I used to go to work very early on Sunday mornings. During the winter months, it would still be quite dark when I arrived. The parking lot was never lit and usually empty when I got in. Even so, I always drove through it as if it were full of cars, taking the same route to my usual parking place.

One morning, I felt a certain lightness about me. It is difficult to explain, but it made me want to get into my spot quicker than usual, so I drove straight through the middle of the parking lot.

Later in the day, a customer came in and asked who he should notify about the hole in the parking lot. When I looked outside, I saw a hole—four foot wide and seven feet

Angels Everywhere

deep—in the area I always drove through. It was definitely big enough to swallow my little compact car.

Looking back, only God knows how badly I would have been hurt, driving along and hitting the bottom of that sink hole. Thankfully though, that Sunday, buoyed by my Guardian Angel's lightness, I made it through okay.

—Ms. Merrill Millwater
Glen Head, N.Y.

An Angel In White

My son Sean had been forbidden to ride his bike without a helmet. However, Sean being Sean, took every opportunity he could to ride without it.

He was visiting his father for the summer when I received a call that he had been hurt and was going into emergency surgery. I lived 2 hours away and the entire trip I just kept praying, "Please let him be okay. . . please, *please* God let him be okay."

When I arrived at the hospital he was already in surgery. He had wrecked his bike and there was a hole in his skull—made when he landed on the bike pedal. The doctors had to remove bone fragments and make a plug to fill in the hole.

Angels Everywhere

When he came out of recovery they allowed me to see him in ICU. I was stunned at his appearance. His face was so swollen it was almost round. He had cuts, bruises, and road rash everywhere. I couldn't believe this was caused by a bike. It looked more like he had been hit by a truck.

When he woke up I gave him a hug and he whispered, "Are you mad?" Unable to speak I shook my head *no*. "Mom, I have to talk to you. . . alone."

The nurses left the room and I whispered, "I love you, tell me anything."

He looked up at the ceiling and speaking in a shaky weak voice said, "I saw an angel. He saved me, Mom."

I was quiet and not sure what to say to him. He said, "It's okay if you don't believe me. But it's true."

I told him that it wasn't that I didn't believe him, it was just that I was surprised. I asked him if he wanted to tell me about it.

"I was riding my bike and there's a grass hill at the park that makes a great jump. When you go over the top of it, you feel like you are flying. You have to be careful though, because there is a parking lot right on the other side and if you are going too fast you'll hit a wood rail on the ground that stops the cars from going on the grass. If you hit it square you can jump it, Mom. I've done it so many times.

Angels Everywhere

"This time I guess I was going too fast or my tire hit it wrong. One second I was flying and the next I hit hard. I knew I was hurt. My head hurt so bad and I felt sick. Then I touched it. Blood was all over my hand. Mom I just lost it, I started screaming, 'Help Me! Help Me!' But no one was there. I tried to stand up but I was so dizzy I fell back down.

"Then I looked up and a man was coming over the hill. He was wearing all white. White pants, white shirt. But he was so dirty Mom, *really* dirty. He had black hair and a mustache. He came over to me and kneeled down and said, 'You will be ok, Sean.'

"I thought, *how can he know my name?* He took off his shirt and bunched it up and tried to put it on my head. I did not want him to put the dirty shirt on my head because it hurt, and tried to push his hand away. He said, 'It's okay, I'm here to help you.' Then he carried me to a spot under a tree and held the shirt to my head.

"When the abulance got there, the EMT's came running. As they were putting me in the ambulance, I looked for the guy who helped me but he was gone. I pulled the shirt from my head and looked at it but now it was clean—so white that it hurt my eyes. It didn't even have blood on it! It was clean—pure white."

Angels Everywhere

I was crying as the full impact of what my son told me hit me. My son had been saved. I held him close and whispered, "Never forget this, Sean. So many people live their whole lives wondering if there really is a God. You have been given proof that there is. Never, never forget this."

I tried to get the shirt that Sean had told me about, but nobody could find it. They thought it must have been thrown out in the ER.

We never found out who had called 911 either. The tape was of a man's voice but he didn't give his name. The recording said, "A child has been hurt on his bike and needs immediate help." He gave the location and hung up. I went on to check with the paramedics but they said Sean was alone under the tree when they arrived.

I know an angel sent by God saved my son's life that day. I know. I believe. . . in angels.

—*Delight Aylesworth*
San Jose, California

Be Good and True

When I was a young girl, I once woke up around 5 a.m. to find a figure standing at the foot of my bed. He was gold and orange, surrounded by a brilliant glow. It was much like the same kind of glow you'd see around clouds during a sunset.

As I looked at him, I was not afraid. Instead, I just stared at him, feeling safe and secure the whole time.

He began speaking to me, and although I do not to this day remember what he said, I remember nodding, taking in everything he told me. I knew then he was my Guardian Angel.

I have been a full-time job for him ever since. I was in a head-on collision with a drunk driver going 70 mph.

Angels Everywhere

Even though I was not wearing a seatbelt (something everyone should do), I walked away with only bumps and bruises.

Another time, I was in a riding accident. The horse fell, and all 700 pounds of him rolled over me. Again, I walked away with no injury.

I was even held up at gunpoint and still managed to avoid any harm. Throughout that and numerous other close calls, I have been convinced that my Guardian Angel was there, standing in the way of danger.

I have seen him only once since that appearance back in my youth. The night I met my husband-to-be, my golden Guardian Angel returned. This time, I heard him plainly and remember every word he spoke.

He told me, "Be good and true and you shall know love for the rest of your life."

His light and his warmth filled me with peace as it had done so long ago. "Every moment won't be glorious, but try to understand what your mate goes through, and love him the way you know is true."

Then he vanished. His words though, have stayed with me ever since. My husband calls me *his* Angel now, and that is a nickname I will live by happily.

—*Kristi Heimrich*
Las Vegas, Nevada

The Old Rabbi

In 1974, my husband and I were in a small Maryland drugstore with our two young sons. We both noticed the loud coughing of an old man who was bent and frail.

We looked at each other in concern — our youngest was very susceptible to respiratory illness and we both had the thought that he shouldn't be near this man.

The man came closer, and despite my fears for my son, I wanted to ask him if he was all right.

He was well dressed and neat, with a coat appropriate for the cold evening, but seemed lost and lonely.

I asked if he was okay. He said he needed to go back home and that he lived in a Hebrew home not far away. A store employee offered to make a phone call for him but the old man replied that it was so close that he would just walk there.

My husband and I agreed that he was too frail to walk even a few blocks in the bitter cold. So, in spite of our fear about exposing our boy to his hacking cough, we offered him a ride home. He accepted.

On the short ride, he spoke eloquently about our kindness. He said he was a rabbi and gave a blessing to each of our children. He was no longer so frail looking and seemed far from sick or senile. We were touched by his words and felt a thrill, like we were experiencing something extraordinary.

The rest of the way home, we talked about Angels, and both believed that we encountered one there, exchanging a simple act of kindness for a blessing.

Many times I have thought about the blessing bestowed on the boys by the rabbi that night. The words were, of course, in Hebrew, spoken in soothing song-like rhythm. He didn't say a lot, but I still feel the strength of it.

There wasn't any dramatic change in the boys' health after the rabbi's blessing, but I do remember feeling deeply concerned about their spiritual well-being. I was agnostic and very disenchanted with religion. I told myself that people had created God — that we used stories about God to smooth over all the rough, unfathomable things we couldn't understand. Religion was just a lullaby we used to soothe ourselves to sleep. I was never certain or happy with these conclusions, but content to drift along.

But my boys! Was it fair to raise them without any spiritual foundation? After meeting the rabbi, I couldn't rest on this issue.

I finally decided that it would be good to at least take them to church so they could learn the stories and they could make up their own minds someday.

It is hard to describe what it was like the first Sunday I walked into a church — announcing that I was just bringing them to Sunday school, and *yes* I guess I would sit in a class for the hour since I would have to wait somewhere.

Well, as you can guess, I went back (for the kids, of course) over and over.

Eventually, I recognized how God was pulling me back to him. I accept now that I will never understand God — religion will always be a mystery, and my questions will remain unanswered in this life. There is no doubt, though, that God is real and powerful and that he loves each of us with an intensity we cannot to comprehend. My husband, amazed at the transformations in my attitude and at how happy I was, started coming to church. Soon he was baptized, too.

My little boys grew up learning about God's love and also chose to believe. A daughter came later — she too is a Christian, and now our youngest, David, has joined the ranks. He is so insightful about the things of God that our pastor believes he'll be a pastor, too, someday.

I'm grateful that God sent an Angel to spur me into thinking about giving my children a chance to know Him.

He could have sent a bolt of lightning.

—Deborah Lane
Lexington, Kentucky

An Answer to Prayer

Iwas on my way to my sister's house. She had moved recently, and I had been to her house only once before. I turned onto her street and after a couple of miles, realized I had made a wrong turn. I was on a two-lane asphalt road with ditches on either side. On the right was forest; on the left, an eight-foot high chain link fence topped with barbed wire surrounded a junkyard with no building or gate in sight. Because there were no intersections or drives in which to turn around, I attempted a three-point turn in the road.

As I was turning, the road caved in underneath me and the front of my car went into the ditch. I was driving a 1984 Camaro Z28 with a HO engine (both large and powerful).

Angels Everywhere

The car was positioned so the back passenger tire (power tire) was off the ground and the middle of the vehicle was bottomed out on the road.

I tried several times to back out, but I was stuck. There was nowhere for me to go and no one in sight to help. Out of nowhere, a man appeared. He was shabbily dressed, about 6 feet tall and slightly built, in his early 30s, with light brown skin and a beard. He asked me to get in my car. He went down into the ditch and placed his hands on the hood. He then told me to back the car out. I started to tell him I had already tried, but he commanded me to back the car out. I threw it in reverse and hit the gas. As easily as could be, the car was back on the road. No man could have picked up the front of that car or pushed it out, but this guy did it effortlessly.

I offered him money and a ride. He turned both down and asked me to "praise God." I got into my car and then got right back out to ask him again to give me the opportunity to pay him, but he'd vanished. Maybe he was just a bum who happened to have superhuman strength and who didn't need money, but I believe he was an Angel.

—*James Tremain*
Houston, Texas

And as I prayed, Gabriel, who I had
seen in a vision, flew to me, and said,
"I have come to help you and to give
you insight into Gods plan. . .
for He loves you dearly.

—*Daniel 9:21*

And I saw seraphim flying over the throne of the Lord, each one calling out to one another saying, "Holy, holy, holy. . ."

—Isaiah 6:3

The Detour

I was working at a downtown law firm in Oklahoma City as the records manager and a messenger. One of my duties was stopping by the post office for the mail on my way in.

This particular morning, I was running late. Upon exiting the interstate I began having a little tug-of-war with myself. If I went straight in, I'd get to work on time. If I stopped, I would be late. Finally, I chose to go to the post office. As I negotiated the one-way streets to get to the post office, I heard a voice say, "Go to the office. You can check the mail later."

I'm not the kind of person who hears voices, but when I heard this one, it was just in time to make the last turn before committing to the one-way only route to the post office. I turned before really even thinking about it and headed to work.

I arrived at work just in time to hear a tremendous explosion and feel a powerful jolt shake the building. The Alfred P. Murray Federal Building had been bombed. All of a sudden it hit me. If I had gone for the mail, I would have been at ground zero when the bomb went off. Thanks to my Guardian Angel, I am here today and don't intend to waste the days I have left. I should have died, but I am blessed to think that I have a chance to do some wonderful things for others.

—*Jay*
 Oklahoma City,
 Oklahoma

The Crossing Guard

I left for work at the usual time and walked the same route I took every day. I was lost in thought as I reached the crosswalk. The car nearest me stopped, so I hurried on my way.

As I stepped into the second lane I felt a pair of strong hands take hold of me and pull me back. As I flew backward, a car came speeding by, just a few centimeters from my body. It didn't even slow down as it blew through the intersection. If I hadn't have been pulled back, I would have been killed.

I looked back to see who had saved me, but there was no one there.

—Angela Anchor
Wichita, Kansas

Faith doesn't get you around problems, it takes you through them.

—*Sign on a church*

You Never Know

We were on our way to a Promise Keepers meeting 1,200 miles away, thinking we would turn this occasion into a family vacation while we were at it. Promise Keepers, for those who don't know, is an event where thousands of men gather in a stadium to pray and recommit themselves to God and to their families. It's a powerful time of fellowship with other Christian men that leaves nearly everyone who attends changed for the better.

My husband was eager to go and so we packed up the car and our three daughters and started for Maryland.

We had put over 800 miles behind us, and were marveling at how well the kids were behaving when our car broke down.

Angels Everywhere

Here we were, hundreds of miles from home and hundreds of miles from our destination, sitting on the side of the road.

We called a tow truck and waited for help. As we sat there, we prayed for God to give us a hand.

The tow truck operator arrived, and we were happy to discover that he, too, was a Christian. We talked about church and Promise Keepers as we made the 40-mile trip to the service station.

Upon our arrival, the mechanic said it was a $60 repair. We were relieved because we figured we could afford that much . As we sat there and waiting, a man came in to have his car worked on as well.

His name was Dan and he was a nice man that seemed to warm up to my husband instantly. Like an old friend he listened to our plans and he seemed genuinely interested in how we were doing.

About then we got some bad news. The repairs would be $600. To make matters worse (and even more expensive) the mechanic would need another day to get the parts which would mean spending the night at a motel. This was far more than we could afford both financially and emotionally.

As my husband went outside to pray, Dan pulled out his credit card and paid the bill. When my husband discovered what had happened, tears filled his eyes as he shook Dan's hand. About then, a friend of Dan's named Russ arrive. He loaded us into a van and took us to a nearby hotel where again, the bill was paid.

I looked up at Russ and asked, "Have you ever seen that show 'Touched by an Angel'?"

He smiled, and said "Why do you ask?"

"I was just wondering if you were an Angel."

He grinned, winked and said, "You never know."

Dan smiled too and said, "You go ahead and enjoy the rest of your trip. Everything is going to be all right."

That night when we said our prayers, we thanked God for all He had done for us. You see, even though bad things were happening to us, God was right there making sure ALL our needs were met. It is so true, He NEVER does leave you nor forsake you.

—Denise Becker
Monticello, Minnesota

The wings I see
Are tinged with gold
Time is endless
Or so I'm told
Feathery white
I know you're there
In my heart
I know you care
Over your shoulder
here we are
Staying close
Never far
Wrap me up
Envelope me
I need you Angel
Can't you see?
Shield me now
Within your wing
Songs of joy
We'll always sing
Hold me tight
And take me high
You belong to me
In my sky
Protect
And love
And nurture me
I need you Angel
Can't you see?

—John Cameron

Saved By An Angel

My friend was hiking in the Sierra Nevada mountains with his two daughters. One was about three and the other was just a baby sitting happily in a backpack baby carrier. They started walking around a reservoir when the three year old said she wanted to play in the water. Her father explained the sides were too steep to stand on. The water also got deep very quickly and she did not know how to swim.

In less than a minute, the beautiful day turned into a nightmare as the three year old tripped and rolled down the steep bank into the water. She struggled but with each panicked move was swept farther out. With the baby still on his back, my friend raced to the water. He reached as far as he could but the little girl was out of reach and moving away from shore.

Desperate, he stepped into with water up to his waist. His feet slipped on the reservoir bottom. He was up to his shoulders now with his daughter still just inches out of his reach. He got his foothold again and stretched once more. Just as he grasped her hand, he slipped again but managed to cling to the girl. He and the baby went under. He kicked with all his might but couldn't get his head above the water. He felt they all three would drown and he desperately prayed, "God, help me!"

Raising a desperate hand to stroke toward shore, he felt a strong hand grasp his. He was yanked with his two daughters out of the water and up the 10 feet to the land above the reservoir.

My friend was laying there holding his daughters and quickly turned over to see who had miraculously saved him. No one was there. The shore was empty. He knew then, that they had been saved by an Angel. God had heard his prayer.

—Duane Brannon
Independence Missouri

Miracle in the Middle of the Night

When I was just 8, I fell ill. I complained for a couple of hours about a headache and had a cough and fever. Mom gave me some medicine and put me to bed early. She was planning on taking me to the doctor first thing in the morning.

Late that night, my sister, who was only 3, came into my room and tried to wake me. When she couldn't, she rushed to my parents and told them. They found me pale, limp, sweating and gasping for air. My lips were blue, so they knew I could not breathe. Dad called for an ambulance.

I was treated for several days with antibiotics and have a scar on my neck where they performed a tracheotomy so I could breathe. The doctors told my mother she was lucky I was still alive. They also told her she was smart to have checked on me and realized I needed hospitalization. Then it hit everyone. When they questioned my sister about it, she said she was awakened by her Angel.

"My Angel said, 'Your brother is sick and he needs you'." She went on to describe how the Angel was lit with a soft glow and guided her down the dark hallway to my room. My sister still remembers the Angel's face and the night the two of them together saved my life.

—Bradley Williams
Ft. Lauderdale Florida

What the Deaf One Heard

I have been deaf all of my life, but I tell you the truth when I say that I can hear the songs of Angels.

The first time I heard them, I was in the hospital. I was a small boy and had just gone through an operation in which doctors attempted to give me hearing. When the operation was over, the surgeon came into the room to explain to my parents that there was no way to correct this problem.

As he was talking to my Mom and Dad, I heard this wonderful noise. It was beautiful and comforting and warm. Then I began to see this light that came in flashes and sparkles, like the sun off of water, shimmering around the figures of Angels. They were invisible to everyone else, but I saw them clearly.

Angels Everywhere

After that, I began to question whether they were really angels I saw that day, but years later at a friends' house, they returned to me. Although I verified with my friend that she couldn't hear a sound, I could hear them again. The light came back too and so did this mist that seemed to swirl and flow around them. I could see their robes, and a glow that outlined them. I go back there often now and enjoy being in their company.

The music they sing is unlike anything I can describe, but I can say that if you have not heard it, you have a treat waiting for you in heaven. It is clear and powerful and it stirs the soul.

I now know Angels are everywhere. They stand outside the door and sit beside you in the library. Sometimes they are someone you have just met and other times they walk right past you at a park sharing only a quick smile. Sometimes though, they are with me, singing a song that only the deaf one hears.

—*Bob Silverman*
Winnetka, California

Behold, I send an Angel before thee, to keep thee in the way, and to bring thee into the place which I have prepared.

—*God*
    Exodus 23:20 KJV

An angel can illume the thought and mind of man by stretching the power of vision, and by bringing within his reach some truth which the angel himself contemplates.

—*St. Thomas Aquinas*

The Blue-eyed Angel

Back in 1997, I was a single girl, out of work and pregnant. I had considered giving my baby up for adoption and even had a nice couple picked out in New York who I thought would make great parents.

Once I decided to give the baby up though, I became quite depressed and found it difficult to function. I kept wrestling with my feelings and wondering about what really was best for me and my unborn child.

❧

One dark and dismal day when I was vacuuming my trailer, I noticed a glow at the end of the hallway. The light got brighter with each second until it became almost blinding.

I walked into the light, squinting to see what the cause of this was. As I got closer, I saw a toddler with white curly hair and big blue eyes, sitting in the center of all that illumination. The baby wore a diaper so I couldn't tell whether it was a boy or a girl.

As my eyes filled with tears, the baby stretched out its arms and started to run toward me. I was so overwhelmed that I fell to the floor sobbing. When I looked up again, the light and the baby were gone.

I knew then that an Angel had given me this chance to see what I would be missing if I gave my child up. Right then and there I changed my mind, and on October 16, I gave birth to a baby boy with white curly hair and big blue eyes.

I'm so glad I kept him and I still cry when he reaches out to hug me.

—Nichole Ohagan
Oklahoma City,
Oklahoma

Miracle—News at 11

I was ready to collapse when I got home from my job where I worked second shift. Although I was exhausted, I was too tense to sleep and decided to read to help me wind down.

The book on my night stand was about true-life Angel stories. I opened it and realized I had read everything except the introduction. It talked about people being in the right place at exactly the right time and how many people pass these miraculous moments off as coincidences. Little did I know I was about to experience such a thing.

Saturday morning, my 3-year-old, Eric, shook me awake, saying something about fire. I assumed he was talking about something on television and rolled over. He persisted and I eventually awoke. Smoke.

As soon as I smelled it, I jumped out of bed, looking for its source. Eric's room was on fire. I got Eric out first, and then went back for my 8-month-old daughter. Her bed was in the back of the apartment but as I went through the front door, I discovered smoke had filled the place. I ran outside, screaming for help. Suddenly, a police car cruised by the building and stopped. The officer saw the smoke and ran toward me.

"Is anyone still inside?" he asked.

"Yes, my daughter. She's in her room — three doors to the left!" I said. He stood there for a moment as if frozen, then dove headlong into the smoke. Several moments went by as the smoke billowed out. I realized in horror I had given him the wrong directions — her room was the second door on the right!

I stood there helplessly wondering if my daughter and this police officer were dying just beyond the wall of smoke. Abruptly, he appeared with my daughter in his arms. We raced down the stairs as fire trucks pulled up with an ambulance. My children were both fine. The paramedics treated me for burns as I watched the roof become engulfed in flame.

Angels Everywhere

A few days later, the police officer came to visit. We talked about that night and I listened as his part of the story unfolded. He said he had never been in our area before, but thought he would do some radar detection near our complex. When he saw the fire, he said he was frightened. When he came to the door of the burning building, he knew he was probably going to die. He said as he hesitated, trying to get his feet to move, he felt a shove in his back. I recalled his dive into the smoke and remembered how strange it seemed for him to go in that way.

He went on to say he followed my directions, going through the wrong door. Overcome by smoke and realizing the little girl wasn't there, he turned to leave but he heard a small cry. He felt himself directed to the right room, grabbed her and left.

News stations sent out camera crews and he was publicly acknowledged for his selfless act of bravery. He was our hero, and we will be forever grateful for him and for the Guardian Angel who showed him the way.

—Martha Ann Michel
Lewiston Maine

WHISPER OF ANGEL WINGS

Today I stumbled and once again

Was lifted up by an unseen hand.

What comfort and joy that knowledge brings.

For I hear the whisper of angel wings.

The guardian angels God sends to all

To bear us up when we stumble and fall.

Trust Him, my friend, and often you'll hear

The whisper of angel wings hovering near.

—Author unknown